D1538847

Goats on the Farm
by Mari C. Schuh

Consulting Editor: Gail Saunders-Smith, Ph.D.

Consultant: Cary J. Trexler, Assistant Professor,
Department of Agricultural Education and Studies,
Iowa State University

Pebble Books

an imprint of Capstone Press
Mankato, Minnesota

Pebble Books are published by Capstone Press
151 Good Counsel Drive, P.O. Box 669, Mankato, Minnesota 56002
http://www.capstone-press.com

1 2 3 4 5 6 07 06 05 04 03 02

Library of Congress Cataloging-in-Publication Data
Schuh, Mari C., 1975–
    Goats on the farm / by Mari C. Schuh.
    p. cm.—(On the farm)
    Includes bibliographical references (p. 23) and index.
    Summary: Photographs and simple text depict the lives of goats on a farm.
    ISBN 0-7368-1188-5
    1. Goats—Juvenile literature. [1. Goats.] I. Title. II. Series.
SF383.35 .S34   2002
636.3'9—dc21   2001004827

Note to Parents and Teachers

The On the Farm series supports national science standards related to life science. This book describes and illustrates goats and their lives on the farm. The photographs support early readers in understanding the text. The repetition of words and phrases helps early readers learn new words. This book also introduces early readers to subject-specific vocabulary words, which are defined in the Words to Know section. Early readers may need assistance to read some words and to use the Table of Contents, Words to Know, Read More, Internet Sites, and Index/Word List sections of the book.

Table of Contents

horns

tail

beard

hooves

Goats live on farms.

buck

doe with kid

A male goat is a buck. A female goat is a doe. Young goats are called kids.

Farmers raise goats for their milk, meat, and wool.

Farmers feed hay
and grain to goats.

Goats graze. They eat grass and other plants.

Goats chew their cud.

Goats live outside during warm weather. Some goats live in barns during cold weather.

Goats climb.

Goats bleat.

Words to Know

bleat—to make a sound like a goat; when a goat bleats, it sounds like "maa."

buck—a male goat; a buck also is called a billy.

cud—food that has not been fully digested; goats bring up food from their stomach to chew; then they swallow the food after it has been chewed again.

doe—a female goat; a doe also is called a nanny; both male and female goats can have horns.

graze—to eat grass and other plants; goats also eat berries, bushes, trees, and weeds.

milk—a white liquid that female goats produce; goat milk is used to make cheese, cottage cheese, ice cream, and sherbet.

wool—the soft, thick, curly hair of some goats; angora goats and some other goats are raised for their wool.

Read More

Hansen, Ann Larkin. *Goats.* Farm Animals. Minneapolis: Abdo & Daughters, 1998.

Miller, Sara Swan. *Goats.* A True Book. New York: Children's Press, 2000.

Wolfman, Judy. *Life on a Goat Farm.* Life on a Farm. Minneapolis: Carolrhoda Books, 2001.

Internet Sites

Breeds of Livestock: Goat Breeds
http://www.ansi.okstate.edu/breeds/goats

Goat
http://www.enchantedlearning.com/subjects/
mammals/goat/goatprintout.shtml

Goats
http://www.ces.ncsu.edu/lenoir/staff/jnix/
pubs/an.workbook/goat.html

Kids Farm: Goats
http://www.kidsfarm.com/goats.htm

Index/Word List

barns, 17
bleat, 21
buck, 7
chew, 15
climb, 19
cold, 17
cud, 15
doe, 7
eat, 13
farmers, 9, 11

farms, 5
feed, 11
female, 7
grain, 11
grass, 13
graze, 13
hay, 11
kids, 7
live, 5, 17
male, 7

meat, 9
milk, 9
outside, 17
plants, 13
raise, 9
warm, 17
weather, 17
wool, 9
young, 7

Word Count: 67
Early-Intervention Level: 9

Credits
Heather Kindseth, cover designer; Heidi Meyer, production designer;
Kimberly Danger and Deirdre Barton, photo researchers

Capstone Press/Gary Sundermeyer, cover, 1, 4, 8, 10, 14
International Stock/George Ancona, 6 (bottom)
Photo Agora/Larry & Rebecca Javorsky, 12
Unicorn Stock Photos/Joel Dexter, 6 (top); Martha McBride, 18
Visuals Unlimited/Inga Spence, 16; Gustav Verderber, 20

Pebble Books thanks Vicki Fleming of Elysian, Minn.; Robert and Sherry Panuska of
New Richland, Minn.; and DeDe Barton of Elysian, Minn., for their assistance with
this book.